The Wisdom of
Emotional Healing

Renowned Psychics
Andrew Jackson Davis and Phineas P. Quimby
Reveal Mind Body Healing Secrets for
Clairvoyants, Spiritualists, and Energy Healers

Rev. Jamie L. Saloff

Sent Books
P. O. Box 339
Edinboro, PA 16412

LCCN: 2010907085
ISBN: 978-0-9740642-7-7
Typography: Nueva Std.
Graphics ©2010 iStockphoto/HiDesigns Graphics

v. 2.0

Second Edition, 2017
First Edition, 2010
Printed on acid free paper.

Visit the author's website:
www.MarvelousMessages.com

For

Tom Cratsley,

Elaine and Mark Thomas,

Cindy Hudson,

the Fellowships of the Spirit staff,

and my FOTS classmates

who walked with me on this journey.

Foreword

This work began quite a few years ago when I first discovered the Phineas Parkhurst Quimby writings. The Quimby writings intrigued me because Quimby had demonstrated in practice what I had written about in theory—how our ailments are founded in our beliefs and emotions and, if one can alter those beliefs, they can engender great and tremendous healing. Quimby proved this through years of private practice with over 12,000 clients, where crutches were left behind, tumors were dissolved, the bedridden rose up from their beds, and thousands of the infirm became well. Quimby not only healed in person, but via written missives to those who could not manage to see him in person.

One of Quimby's patients, Mary Baker Eddy, later used ideas from Quimby's curing method as the basis for Christian Science. Quimby supporters claimed she sidestepped the true foundation of Quimby's healing method, as did other religious offsprings, such as New Thought. Quimby adamantly never wanted a religion created from his beliefs, often writing against religious groups and blaming their dogma for causing many of the day's ailments.

Phineas Parkhurst Quimby:
February 16, 1802—January 16th, 1866

For me, Quimby's writings were laced with the problem that they were archaic, written in the late 1800s, and not in the least easy to understand. In fact, from a writer and book publishing consultant's point of view, Quimby's writing could be called atrocious, often changing tenses within a paragraph, skipping around on topics—many times leaving the reader hanging on his initial discussion or abruptly ending mid-sentence as if he'd been called away. Over the years, various biographers and copyists tried to "fix" Quimby's writings by changing punctuation, adding words, or inserting their own interpretations*. It's only been in recent years, one in 2009, that publishers of his works have attempted to display his writings "as written" in an attempt to portray Quimby as he himself had intended. Nevertheless, it is sometimes easier to read the writings of others' explanations, gleaning a better understanding, than it is to attempt to grasp Quimby himself, especially since he writes of high ideas and spiritual concepts, which are difficult for anyone to explain, even now in the twenty-first century.

I kept digging away at the Quimby material, not making much headway. Then, in 2008, while attending Fellowships of the Spirit School of Healing and Prophecy in Lily Dale, New York, we were introduced to

Andrew Jackson Davis:
August 11, 1826 —January 13, 1910

Andrew Jackson Davis. This was the first I'd heard of Davis, but immediately began to see similarities between Davis and Quimby. Instantly, I began to wonder if, at last, I might be able to piece together some of the riddles that had plagued me when reading Quimby's works. Perhaps Davis had presented these concepts more clearly. I set out to learn more.

Andrew Jackson Davis, literally named for the former U.S. president, (this, before the president actually took office), also lived during the 1800s.

*You will see this demonstrated here, as older, public versions are used.

In as many ways that Davis and Quimby shared like ideas in their writings, they also displayed many contrasts. For one, Davis wrote more eloquently, vividly describing heavenly worlds, scientific findings, medical facts, and spiritual occurrences. While Quimby often wrote against the newly formed Spiritualist believers, Davis became one of their spiritual leaders. Quimby typically sat quietly with his patients, or perhaps talked with them, curing by removing hindering emotional beliefs, contrasting Davis who used, at first, a method comparable to that of Edgar Cayce. (In fact, Cayce studied the works of Davis.) Initially, Davis would allow himself to be mesmerized into a trance state by an "operator," then dictated answers to questions to a transcriptionist. In this state, Davis prescribed alternative cures in exacting details to ailing clients. Upon awaking, Davis would remember nothing and, being undereducated, hardly understood what he had prescribed.

After some years, Davis experienced a mind-opening vision, including finding himself miraculously transported some 40 miles from home—an event that defied explanation. Thereafter, Davis could access Wisdom without being mesmerized and had a keen understanding of the all.

Over the period of his life, Davis wrote more than 30 books, the most noteworthy being *The Principles of Nature, The Magic Staff,* and *The Great Harmonia,* the latter consisting of six volumes. He also wrote countless articles for magazines and periodicals, including several that he or his organizations published.

In his lifetime, Quimby never wrote a book, but desired to share his teachings with all in the belief that one day we would all heal "by the words of our mouths," no longer needing the cures of doctors or the forgiveness of priests, which he felt caused more harm than good.

He wrote extensively about not taking to heart the opinions of others, suggesting we look for verifiable facts over heresay. Instead of books, Quimby wrote short essays and pamphlets that he shared with many of his clients and friends. In the last years of his life, he worked with secretary/transcriptionist Annetta G. Dresser to put many of his ideas into words, but all these remained unpublished at his death. Later, these were compiled and published by others, including Dresser's son, Horatio.

I had begun my interest in mesmerism knowing that the process included having an "operator" (or mesmerist) run their hands up and down the body of the seated volunteer. To me, this was the use of modern day-energy medicine in practice, such as that taught by Donna Eden, as well as energy dowsers such as Sig Lonegren and Joseph Korn. Knowing the awesome abilities of these two healers (Davis and Quimby), I expected to learn how I could use mesmerism (or energy medicine) to heal as they did. The first surprise came when I learned both men had thrown off mesmerism for clairvoyance, and then had thrown off clairvoyance for what they referred to as Wisdom (and several other names). Thus, upon realizing the scope of works and depth of the writings of these two wise souls, my goal became to put together a simple book of quotations expressing the core of these men's beliefs in such a way as to cause the reader to seek Wisdom.

This book, then, utilizes quotes from Quimby and Davis, as well as others who wrote about them, in an attempt to share what I learned about Wisdom. It does not, however, do so conclusively, since neither man explained his process explicitly. In fact, they often spoke in riddles, some say purposely coding this path to enlightenment. Therefore, the reader, each by their own means, will be left to find their own meaning in these words, and to search further through the works of yesterday and today to explain them. Many of today's writers have furthered these ideas along different paths. These range from books by Walter Russell to Donna Eden's *Energy Medicine*, includes modalities from NLP to EFT, as well as *A Course in Miracles*. While Davis and Quimby often allude to the instruction of obtaining Wisdom, one often wonders how much of it was up to "Divine Providence" (as Davis calls it)—the favor of God— even though both assure the reader these gifts are available to all.

For my own self, the effect of their writings has been profound. I have been inspired and impassioned to continue reading, continue understanding, and continue searching deeper to better understand the concept that led Davis and Quimby to heal, love, live, give and find joy. Both men, under the influence of Wisdom, carried with them a tremendous faith, integrity, and desire to help others to heal their lives. This did not necessarily make their lives easier, wildly successful, nor did it make them rich. Reportedly, Quimby became ill and eventually died, most claim due to overwork. Davis often found himself the brunt of attack by friend and foe for his beliefs and due to his high profile in the spiritualist community. Nevertheless, it appears to me that their aim, which was to help others heal and uplift their lives, while also being in direct connection to God and the heavenly hosts, would be a pleasing goal for any healer to attain.

Lastly, I did find the answers to several of the personal riddles that I had earlier sought. My family will attest to the very strange day when I burst from my office dancing and giddy, having learned not only that Quimby had left a quote opening a door to my understanding, but that I myself had written a similar explanation of this very riddle in 2004 for my book *Transformational Healing: A Self-Healing Journey Toward Greater Wellness,*

Personal Growth, and Purposeful Living, but had not previously connected the two. (I have included this short piece at the end of the book.) Laughingly, I then lost track of the all-important quote and had to seek it out a second time. (I did find it and included it here.)

In closing, I hope you will soon realize the power of Wisdom and pray that you may find it useful in healing and improving the lives of those around you, as well as your own.

Rev. Jamie L. Saloff
May 2010

How to Read This Book:

Read each of the quotations
as if it is a meditation,
taking a few minutes after each one
to close your eyes
and really absorb what has been said.
(I find it helps, to read one line at a time.)

Allow it to sink into your mind.

Feel it.
Try it on.
Imagine it in action.

Reflect on what it means to you.

You may find some to be quite controversial,
while others are more like a riddle.

Should you want to search deeper and learn more,
a reference section is provided in the back.

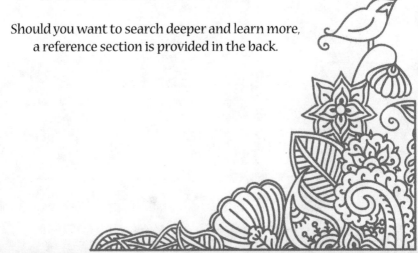

Thoughts on Medicine
and Disease

With today's technologies and research,
it's surprising how very little things have changed
since the nineteenth century.

If medicine is adequate to the curing of disease,
why are chronic diseases so prevalent?

Andrew Jackson Davis
The Great Harmonia, Vol. 1, p. 234

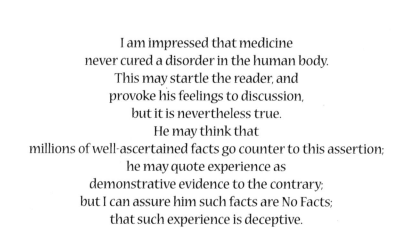

I am impressed that medicine
never cured a disorder in the human body.
This may startle the reader, and
provoke his feelings to discussion,
but it is nevertheless true.
He may think that
millions of well-ascertained facts go counter to this assertion;
he may quote experience as
demonstrative evidence to the contrary;
but I can assure him such facts are No Facts;
that such experience is deceptive.

The contest is never between the Medicine and the Disease;
it is always between Nature and the Medicine.

Andrew Jackson Davis
The Great Harmonia, Vol. 1, p. 234-235

"...all medical remedies affect the body only through the mind."
The one who takes medicine
must believe in medicine
and anticipate the desired result.
The result is then created by the believer.

Horatio Willis Dresser, quoting and paraphrasing
Phineas Parkhurst Quimby
The Quimby Manuscripts, p. 188

5

While priests and clergymen
have supposed themselves divinely commissioned
to heal spiritual or moral infirmities,
physicians have considered their mission
confined to the sphere of physical or visible affliction.
Between these two professions,
the human soul has been unfortunately situated,
admonished,
misrepresented,
and forced into more disease
and misdirection
than it could otherwise have ever known.

...I love to address the masses and professions
which reciprocally injure and support each other.

Andrew Jackson Davis
The Great Harmonia, Vol. 1, p. 215

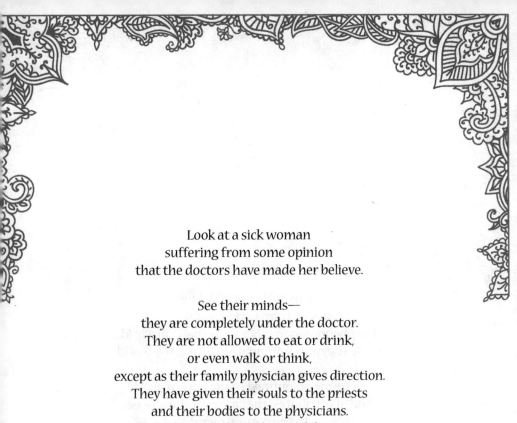

Look at a sick woman
suffering from some opinion
that the doctors have made her believe.

See their minds—
they are completely under the doctor.
They are not allowed to eat or drink,
or even walk or think,
except as their family physician gives direction.
They have given their souls to the priests
and their bodies to the physicians.
They then tell about the good doctor—
how much he has done for them—
showing that he has deprived them of all noble, manly feelings,
and left them sick,
feeble in mind and body....

Annetta G. Dresser, quoting Phineas Parkhurst Quimby
The Philosophy of P. P. Quimby, p. 101

The world is full of sickness,
arising from various causes—
the phenomenon exists in the natural world,
while the causes originate in an *invisible* world.

Doctoring is confined to the natural world,
and [it attributes] the causes of the disease
to the natural world.

Horatio Willis Dresser
The Quimby Manuscripts, p. 191
(*emphasis added*)

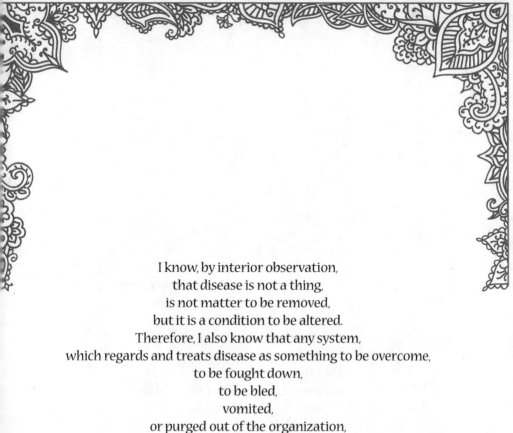

I know, by interior observation,
that disease is not a thing,
is not matter to be removed,
but it is a condition to be altered.
Therefore, I also know that any system,
which regards and treats disease as something to be overcome,
to be fought down,
to be bled,
vomited,
or purged out of the organization,
has its foundation deep in the error of antiquity.

Andrew Jackson Davis
The Great Harmonia, Vol. 1, p. 114

9

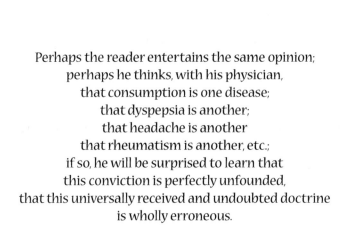

Perhaps the reader entertains the same opinion;
perhaps he thinks, with his physician,
that consumption is one disease;
that dyspepsia is another;
that headache is another
that rheumatism is another, etc.;
if so, he will be surprised to learn that
this conviction is perfectly unfounded,
that this universally received and undoubted doctrine
is wholly erroneous.

(continues...)

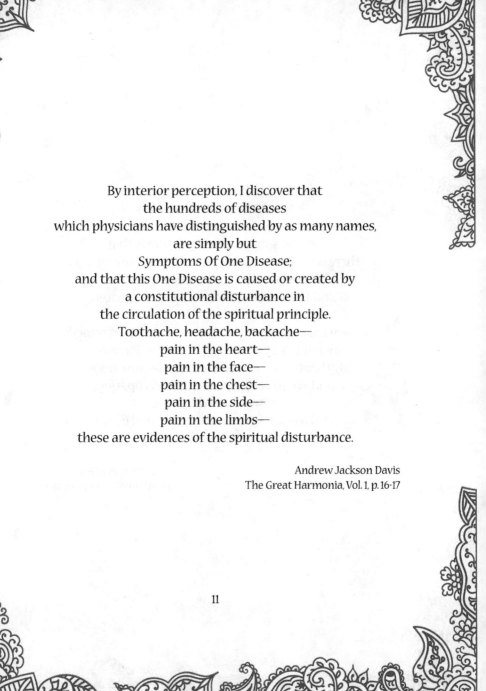

By interior perception, I discover that
the hundreds of diseases
which physicians have distinguished by as many names,
are simply but
Symptoms Of One Disease;
and that this One Disease is caused or created by
a constitutional disturbance in
the circulation of the spiritual principle.
Toothache, headache, backache—
pain in the heart—
pain in the face—
pain in the chest—
pain in the side—
pain in the limbs—
these are evidences of the spiritual disturbance.

Andrew Jackson Davis
The Great Harmonia, Vol. 1, p. 16-17

When I cure,
there is one disease the less;
but not so when others cure,
for the supply of sickness shows that
there is more disease on hand than there ever was.
Therefore, the labor for health is slow,
and the manufacture of disease is greater.

The newspapers teem with advertisements of remedies,
showing that the supply of disease increases.
My theory teaches man to manufacture health;
and, when people go into this occupation,
disease will diminish,
and those who furnish disease and death
will be few and scarce.

Phineas Parkhurst Quimby
The Quimby Manuscripts, p. 35

12

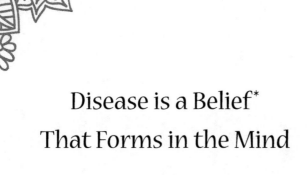

Disease is a Belief[*]
That Forms in the Mind

[*]For more information on how to identify a belief, see my book, *Transformational Healing: Five Surprisingly Simple Keys Designed to Redirect Your Life Toward Wellness, Purpose, and Prosperity*; Chapter 6.

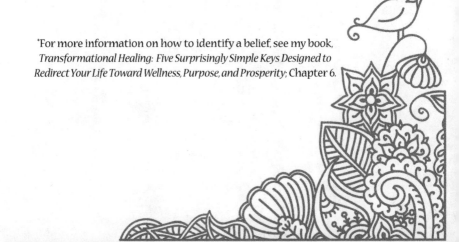

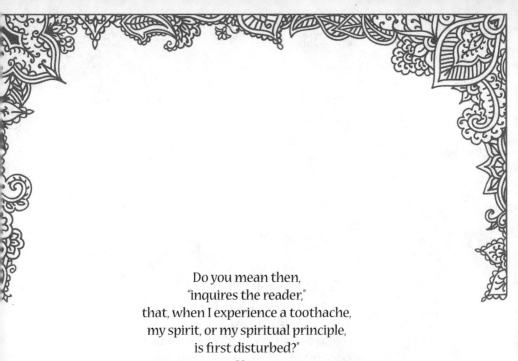

Do you mean then,
"inquires the reader,"
that, when I experience a toothache,
my spirit, or my spiritual principle,
is first disturbed?"
Yes;
if you experience an ache,
or a pain,
or an uneasy sensation,
it is positively certain that your spiritual principle has been,
and is now,
thrown off its proper equilibrium.

Andrew Jackson Davis
The Great Harmonia, Vol. 1, p. 16-17

...Disease may be defined,
from the mental point of view,
as disturbed action.
This definition involves no denial
of the physiological conditions of disease.
It by no means resolves disease into a mere "error."
The point is that,
whatever the physical disability,
the disease is mentally known as
disturbed equilibrium.

Horatio Willis Dresser, Quimby biographer
Health and the Inner Life, p. 236-237

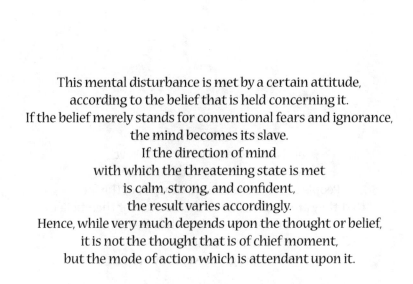

This mental disturbance is met by a certain attitude,
according to the belief that is held concerning it.
If the belief merely stands for conventional fears and ignorance,
the mind becomes its slave.
If the direction of mind
with which the threatening state is met
is calm, strong, and confident,
the result varies accordingly.
Hence, while very much depends upon the thought or belief,
it is not the thought that is of chief moment,
but the mode of action which is attendant upon it.

This is a crucial point that has been
almost invariably overlooked
by mind-cure devotees.

Horatio Willis Dresser, Quimby's biographer
Health and the Inner Life, p. 236-237

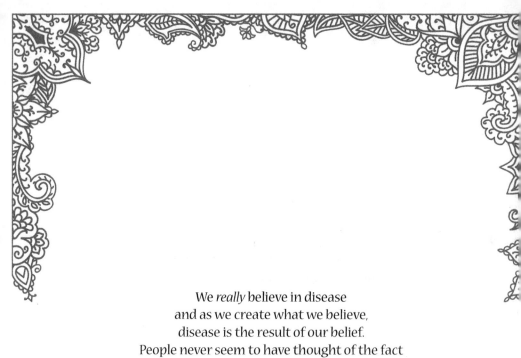

We *really* believe in disease
and as we create what we believe,
disease is the result of our belief.
People never seem to have thought of the fact
that they are responsible to themselves for their belief.
Therefore, to analyze their beliefs
is to know themselves,
which is the greatest study of man.

Phineas Parkhurst Quimby
The Quimby Manuscripts, p. 61 & p. 352
(*emphasis added*)

I found that by the power of my own mind
I could change the mind of my patient
and produce a chemical change in the body,
like dissolving a tumor.

Phineas Parkhurst Quimby
The Quimby Manuscripts, p. 180

When the mind is agitated by fear of receiving any disease,
that moment the body is susceptible
to the invasion of the enemy.
Some minds get panic-struck—
that is, psychologized—
by the apprehension of having an attack of
cholera, plague, small pox, yellow fever, & etc.,
and the consequence is, that,
in five cases out of ten,
the individual is eventually captured
with the disorder most dreaded,
or by some disease very analogous.
The constant fear of heart disease,
of consumption,
or of cancer,
is very likely to induce
the very complaint which is feared.

Andrew Jackson Davis
The Great Harmonia, Vol. 3, p. 98

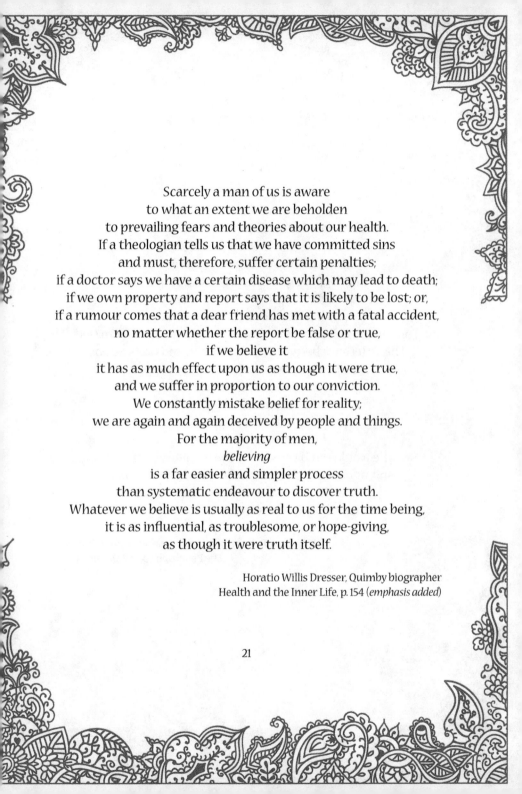

Scarcely a man of us is aware
to what an extent we are beholden
to prevailing fears and theories about our health.
If a theologian tells us that we have committed sins
and must, therefore, suffer certain penalties;
if a doctor says we have a certain disease which may lead to death;
if we own property and report says that it is likely to be lost; or,
if a rumour comes that a dear friend has met with a fatal accident,
no matter whether the report be false or true,
if we believe it
it has as much effect upon us as though it were true,
and we suffer in proportion to our conviction.
We constantly mistake belief for reality;
we are again and again deceived by people and things.
For the majority of men,
believing
is a far easier and simpler process
than systematic endeavour to discover truth.
Whatever we believe is usually as real to us for the time being,
it is as influential, as troublesome, or hope-giving,
as though it were truth itself.

Horatio Willis Dresser, Quimby biographer
Health and the Inner Life, p. 154 (*emphasis added*)

I am often accused
of opposing the medical faculty and the religious creeds.
In answer to this, I plead guilty;
but you must not gather from this
that I oppose goodness or virtue or wisdom.
I oppose all religion which is based on the opinions of men;
and, as God never gave an opinion,
I am not bound to believe that man's opinions are from God.
The difference between man's opinion and God's *wisdom*
is more than one would naturally suppose;
but the *former* is taken for a truth,
and this makes the trouble
with which the wise have to contend.
If man knew himself,
he would not be misled by the opinions of others;
and, as *disease is the result of our knowledge or opinions*,
it is the duty of all to know themselves
that they may correct their own errors.

Annetta G. Dresser, quoting Phineas Parkhurst Quimby
The Philosophy of P. P. Quimby, p. 81
(*emphasis added*)

Now I had resolved to do this woman good.
I appreciated her weakness of mind,
her belief in witchcraft,
and her total ignorance of the fact
that she was merely psychologized by Fear.

Logic,
persuasion,
philosophy,
religion,
was none of them the remedy;
nothing but a psychological power more positive,
applied without explanation,
would cure and save her.
Of this I was morally certain.

Andrew Jackson Davis
The Magic Staff, p. 461

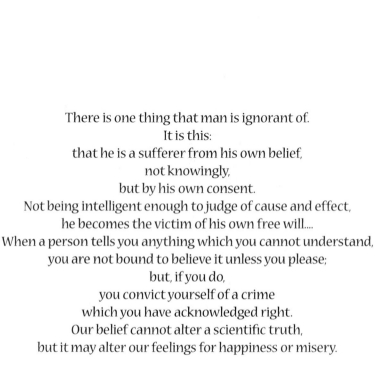

There is one thing that man is ignorant of.
It is this:
that he is a sufferer from his own belief,
not knowingly,
but by his own consent.
Not being intelligent enough to judge of cause and effect,
he becomes the victim of his own free will....
When a person tells you anything which you cannot understand,
you are not bound to believe it unless you please;
but, if you do,
you convict yourself of a crime
which you have acknowledged right.
Our belief cannot alter a scientific truth,
but it may alter our feelings for happiness or misery.

Annetta G. Dresser, quoting Phineas Parkhurst Quimby
The Philosophy of P. P. Quimby, p. 88

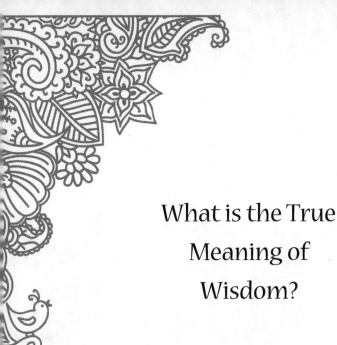

What is the True Meaning of Wisdom?

Before you can find it, try it on, or wear it,
you must first know what you're looking for
and what to expect when you obtain it.

Now to cure you,
or take down the building,
is to show you that
all the feelings that you had at the commencement
arose from trifling cause,
and that, when I can make you understand it,
I have performed the cure.

Instead of giving medicine
or going to work by guess to destroy the building,
I commence by showing the patient
how he framed it by his own hand
or wisdom.

Annetta G. Dresser, quoting Phineas Parkhurst Quimby
The Philosophy of P. P. Quimby, p. 93

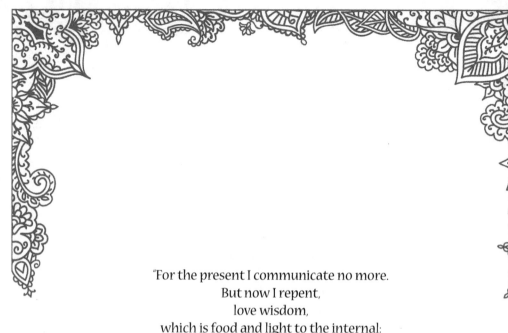

"For the present I communicate no more.
But now I repent,
love wisdom,
which is food and light to the internal:
and wisdom secureth health;
and health procureth happiness.
And thus strengthened, enlightened, and purified,
thou wilt find it congenial to seek
and thirst after
interior and beautiful truths."

Andrew Jackson Davis
relating words spoken to him during a vision
The Magic Staff, p. 244

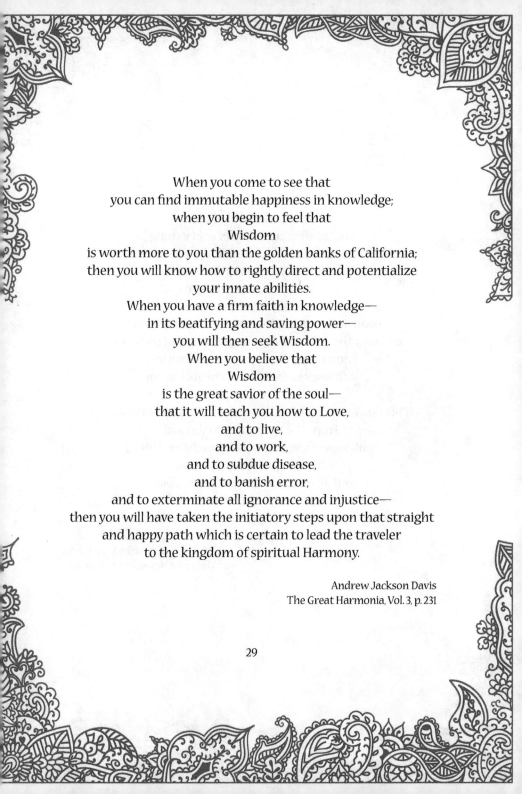

When you come to see that
you can find immutable happiness in knowledge;
when you begin to feel that
Wisdom
is worth more to you than the golden banks of California;
then you will know how to rightly direct and potentialize
your innate abilities.
When you have a firm faith in knowledge—
in its beatifying and saving power—
you will then seek Wisdom.
When you believe that
Wisdom
is the great savior of the soul—
that it will teach you how to Love,
and to live,
and to work,
and to subdue disease,
and to banish error,
and to exterminate all ignorance and injustice—
then you will have taken the initiatory steps upon that straight
and happy path which is certain to lead the traveler
to the kingdom of spiritual Harmony.

Andrew Jackson Davis
The Great Harmonia, Vol. 3, p. 231

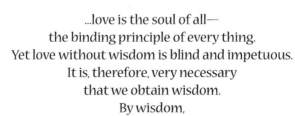

...love is the soul of all—
the binding principle of every thing.
Yet love without wisdom is blind and impetuous.
It is, therefore, very necessary
that we obtain wisdom.
By wisdom,
I mean a strong intuitive understanding of truth,
without the cold and fatiguing process of cogitation,
and wearying our mental faculties
with useless exercises in ratiocination.

This power of truthful discernment will increase in you
from the moment you discard
all superficial habits of thought and life;
become perfectly natural;
and all errors and Supernaturalisms
will pass from your mind,
as clouds glide away from the face of the firmament.

Andrew Jackson Davis
The Great Harmonia, Vol. 3, p. 150

What is health?
I know of no better answer than this:
it is perfect wisdom,
and just as a man is wise in his health;
but as no man is perfectly wise
no man has perfect health.

Phineas Parkhurst Quimby
The Quimby Manuscripts, p. 311

All Truth may be found in Nature,
and in the nature of man,
because God lives in Nature;
therefore, when we study Nature
we study God;
therefore, too, in proportion as we comprehend Nature,
in the same proportion we comprehend God.

Andrew Jackson Davis
The Great Harmonia, Vol. 3, p. 375

If the reader is true to Nature
(which is being true to himself
and to the Divine Mind)
he can improve the condition of his neighbor,
and heal individuals of many apparently incurable maladies.

Let all aspire to this glorious state of spiritual exaltation!

Andrew Jackson Davis
The Great Harmonia, Vol. 1, p. 295

By the immutable action
of his psychological principles
of omnipotence,
the Deity fills the world with life,
which is Love,
and with order,
which is Wisdom.

Andrew Jackson Davis
The Great Harmonia, Vol. 3, p. 103

Wisdom cannot change,
but can arrange and classify ideas
each in its proper place,
and show where mind falls short of wisdom.

To suppose mind is wisdom
is as false as to suppose power is weight.

Phineas Parkhurst Quimby
The Quimby Manuscripts, p. 235

Truth is the same yesterday,
today,
and forever.
It is the same always and everywhere.
Absolute Truth is immutable.
He that teaches a doctrine which is absolutely true,
does not proclaim a thing which is temporarily certain;
but an everlasting substantialism
which rests upon the immutable authority of God.

Andrew Jackson Davis
The Great Harmonia, Vol. 3, p. 363

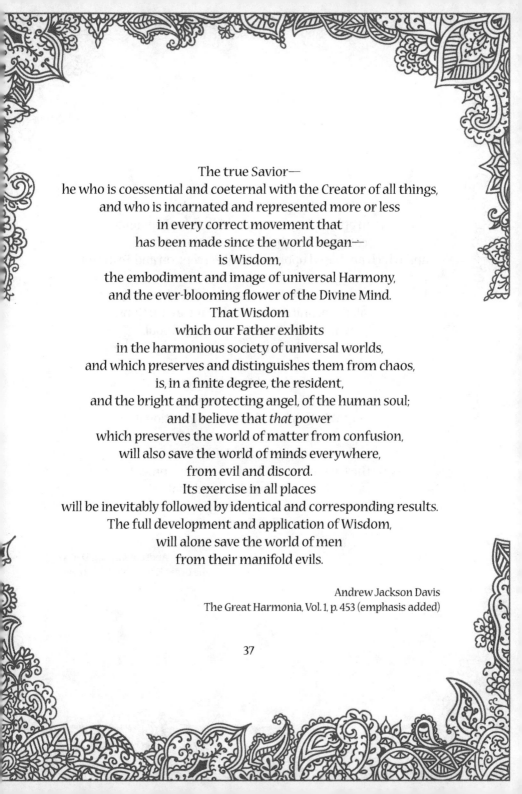

The true Savior—
he who is coessential and coeternal with the Creator of all things,
and who is incarnated and represented more or less
in every correct movement that
has been made since the world began—
is Wisdom,
the embodiment and image of universal Harmony,
and the ever-blooming flower of the Divine Mind.
That Wisdom
which our Father exhibits
in the harmonious society of universal worlds,
and which preserves and distinguishes them from chaos,
is, in a finite degree, the resident,
and the bright and protecting angel, of the human soul;
and I believe that *that* power
which preserves the world of matter from confusion,
will also save the world of minds everywhere,
from evil and discord.
Its exercise in all places
will be inevitably followed by identical and corresponding results.
The full development and application of Wisdom,
will alone save the world of men
from their manifold evils.

Andrew Jackson Davis
The Great Harmonia, Vol. 1, p. 453 (emphasis added)

It is well to understand that Knowledge or Learning,
is an effect of a multitude of facts and opinions
consigned to the recesses of the memory,
and which are based upon external Perception and Testimony;
but Wisdom
is an effect of the full and harmonious development
of all the affinities, affections, and attractions,
which constitute the immortal Soul,
and adorn its fair proportions.

Remember this distinction—
Knowledge is acquired and superficial;
but Wisdom is unfolded and intuitional.

According to this definition of
the two sources of human enlightenment,
it is easy to understand that
reformation in the science of healing and preventing disease
is absolutely necessary.

Andrew Jackson Davis
The Great Harmonia, Vol. 1, p. 216

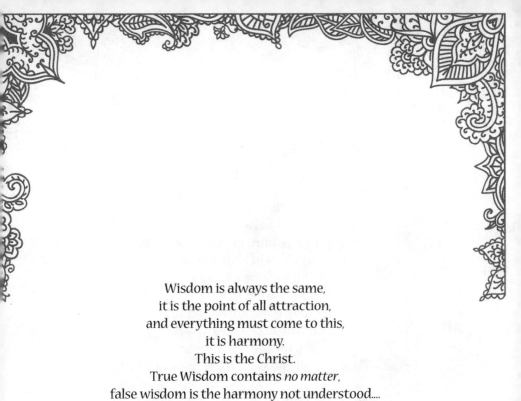

Wisdom is always the same,
it is the point of all attraction,
and everything must come to this,
it is harmony.
This is the Christ.
True Wisdom contains *no matter*,
false wisdom is the harmony not understood....

Wisdom leaves no loophole, it can be tested.

Phineas Parkhurst Quimby
The Quimby Manuscripts, p. 55
(*emphasis added*)

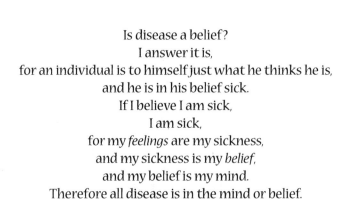

Is disease a belief?
I answer it is,
for an individual is to himself just what he thinks he is,
and he is in his belief sick.
If I believe I am sick,
I am sick,
for my *feelings* are my sickness,
and my sickness is my *belief*,
and my belief is my mind.
Therefore all disease is in the mind or belief.

Now as our belief or disease is made up of ideas,
which are *matter*,
it is necessary to know what beliefs we are in;
for to cure the disease
is to correct the error,
and as disease is what follows the error,
destroy the cause,
and the effect will cease.

Phineas Parkhurst Quimby
The Quimby Manuscripts, p. 185-186

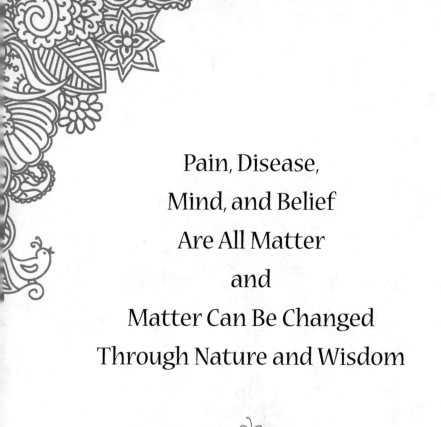

Pain, Disease,
Mind, and Belief
Are All Matter
and
Matter Can Be Changed
Through Nature and Wisdom

Are you willing to change?

Happy [are] they,
who penetrate into internal things,
and endeavor to prepare themselves
more and more
by daily exercises
to the attaining to
heavenly secrets.

Father a'Kempis, as quoted by Andrew Jackson Davis
Views of Our Heavenly Home, p. 14

Ignorance is disease,
although not accompanied by pain.
Pain is not disease itself,
but is what follows disease.
According to my theory,
disease is a belief,
and where there is no fear there can be no pain;
for pain is not the act
but the *reaction* of something which creates pain....

But, says someone,
I never thought of pain 'till it came.
But if it came
something must have started it.
Therefore it must be an effect,
whether it came from some place or from ourselves.
I take the ground that it is generated in ourselves,
and that it must have a cause.

Phineas Parkhurst Quimby
The Quimby Manuscripts, p. 311

Sensation contains no intelligence or belief,
but is a mere disturbance of the matter, called agitation,
which produces *mind*,
and is ready to receive the seed of error.
Ever since man was created,
there has been an element called error
which has been busy inventing answers for every sensation.

Annetta G. Dresser, quoting Phineas Parkhurst Quimby
The Philosophy of P. P. Quimby, p. 88
(*emphasis added*)

It is that spiritual principle within you
which thinks,
feels,
loves,
and reasons—
it is your interior self!

Andrew Jackson Davis
The Philosophy of Spiritual Intercourse, p. 83

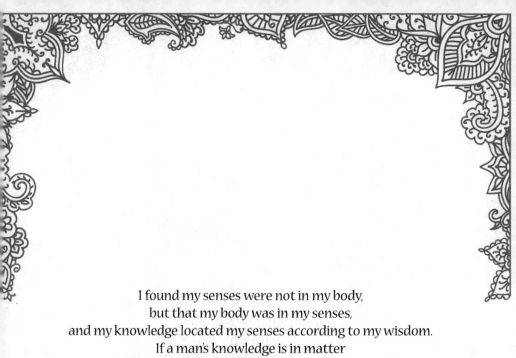

I found my senses were not in my body,
but that my body was in my senses,
and my knowledge located my senses according to my wisdom.
If a man's knowledge is in matter
all there is of him (to him)
is contained in matter.
But if his knowledge is in Wisdom,
then his senses and all there is of him
are *outside* of matter.

Phineas Parkhurst Quimby
The Quimby Manuscripts, p. 245-249

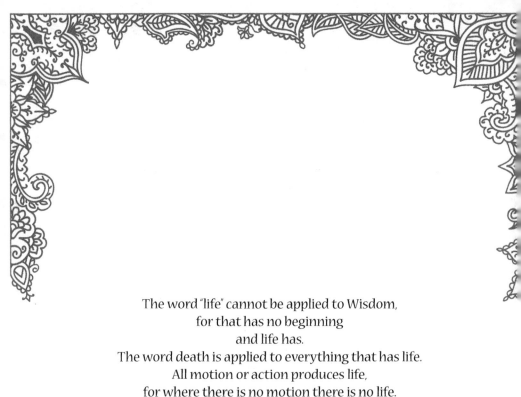

The word "life" cannot be applied to Wisdom,
for that has no beginning
and life has.
The word death is applied to everything that has life.
All motion or action produces life,
for where there is no motion there is no life.
Matter in motion is called life.
Life is the action of matter...

Phineas Parkhurst Quimby
The Quimby Manuscripts, p. 245-249

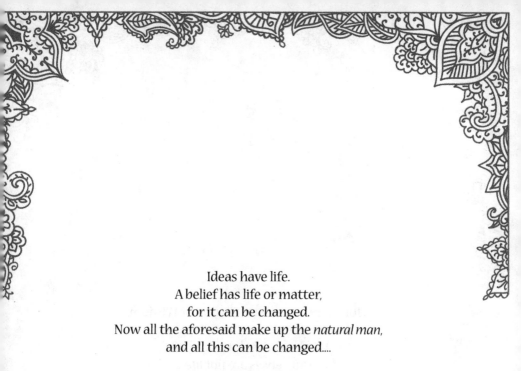

Ideas have life.
A belief has life or matter,
for it can be changed.
Now all the aforesaid make up the *natural man,*
and all this can be changed....

The scientific man makes all sensation
outside of the idea of matter,
so that to him *all sensation*
must be made on something independent
of the natural idea of the senses.

Phineas Parkhurst Quimby
The Quimby Manuscripts, p. 245-254
(emphasis added)

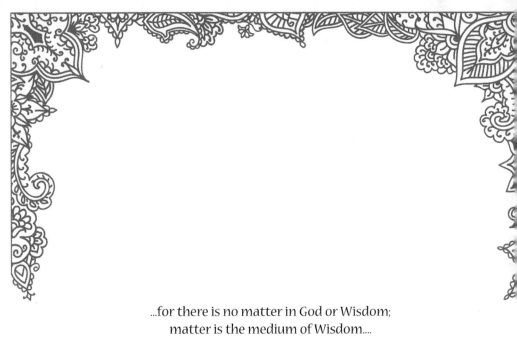

...for there is no matter in God or Wisdom;
matter is the medium of Wisdom....
Wisdom is not [physical] life.
Our senses are not life.
But all of these are solid and eternal;
and to know them
is life and life eternal.

Phineas Parkhurst Quimby
The Quimby Manuscripts, p. 245-249

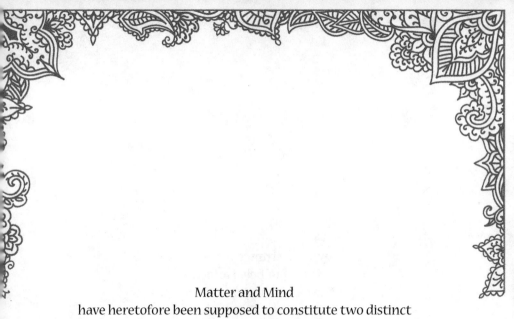

Matter and Mind
have heretofore been supposed to constitute two distinct
and independent substances—
the latter having no material origin.
But it is coming to be seen
that Truth is A Unit,
that Nature is everywhere consistent with herself,
and that mind is the flower of matter,
as man is the flower of creation.

Andrew Jackson Davis
The Great Harmonia, Vol. 3, p. 15

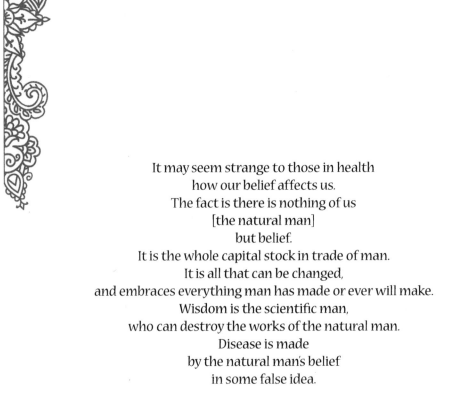

It may seem strange to those in health
how our belief affects us.
The fact is there is nothing of us
[the natural man]
but belief.
It is the whole capital stock in trade of man.
It is all that can be changed,
and embraces everything man has made or ever will make.
Wisdom is the scientific man,
who can destroy the works of the natural man.
Disease is made
by the natural man's belief
in some false idea.

Phineas Parkhurst Quimby
The Quimby Manuscripts, p. 245-249

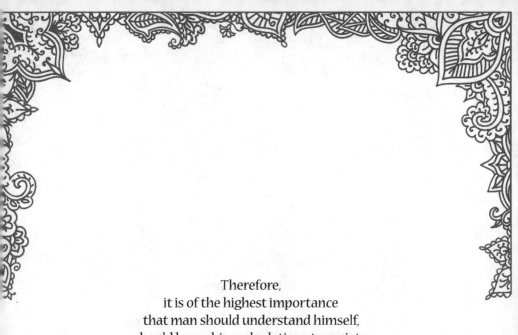

Therefore,
it is of the highest importance
that man should understand himself,
should know his real relations to society,
how he is influenced
and how to overcome the subtle influences
by which he is surrounded;
and to possess this knowledge
is to know this science or wisdom
which separates truth from error.

Annetta G. Dresser,
The Philosophy of P. P. Quimby, p. 59

To know the one
self or kingdom from the other,
to obey and develop the real or spiritual self,
and destroy the self or man of opinions,
is not only to possess,
but to live
the science of life and happiness.
Health and happiness
will come in proportion
as this truth is made vital in daily life.

Annetta G. Dresser
The Philosophy of P. P. Quimby, p. 59

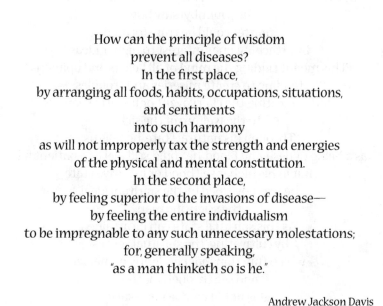

How can the principle of wisdom
prevent all diseases?
In the first place,
by arranging all foods, habits, occupations, situations,
and sentiments
into such harmony
as will not improperly tax the strength and energies
of the physical and mental constitution.
In the second place,
by feeling superior to the invasions of disease—
by feeling the entire individualism
to be impregnable to any such unnecessary molestations;
for, generally speaking,
"as a man thinketh so is he."

Andrew Jackson Davis
The Great Harmonia, Vol. 3, p. 100

...having become convinced that
"matter was only a medium for our wisdom to act through,"
he [Quimby] saw how
matter could be transformed
by attaching one's interest to higher ideas.
This meant ridding the mind of all beliefs and opinions
tending to create miseries and troubles,
and dedicating the clairvoyant or intuitive powers
to the welfare of the sick.
Through his natural state, he tells us,
as a being of flesh and blood, he could still feel as a patient felt.
But in his higher selfhood or intuitive state
he was governed by the spiritual ideal,
"the scientific man."
As this spiritual state can be attained
by cultivating "the spiritual senses,"
which function independently of matter
and see through matter,
it is not of course necessary
to make the body quiescent through the use of mesmerism.

Horatio Willis Dresser, Quimby biographer
quoting and speaking of Phineas Parkhurst Quimby
The Quimby Manuscripts, p. 55

56

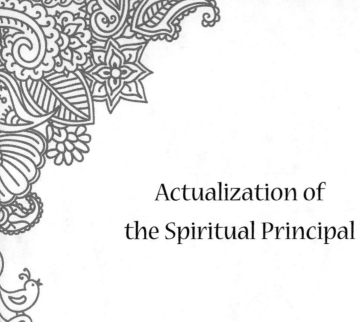

Actualization of
the Spiritual Principal

According to Davis, the Spiritual Principal is the highest spiritual state available to physical man. It was from this state Quimby and Davis were able to heal and gain Wisdom.

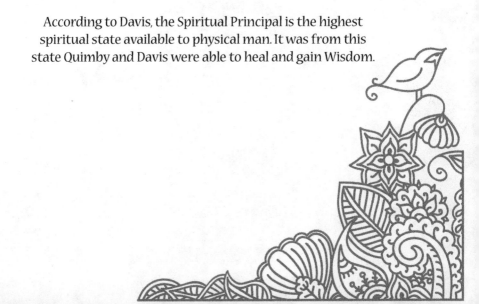

The intelligent individual
needs not
to be informed
that this Age
is one of unparalleled
mental activity.

Andrew Jackson Davis
The Philosophy of Spiritual Intercourse, p. 11

And such is the perfection
and unchangeability
of this great law of universal adaptation,
that it is perfectly safe and reasonable to affirm,
and to also expect,
that when man *wants* miracles
he will assuredly find them;
when he *wants* to see,
and hear,
and converse with spiritual beings,
he may rest satisfied
in the belief that his desire has,
somewhere in the great providential allotments
of God's immutable laws
its complete and appropriate
gratification!

Andrew Jackson Davis
The Philosophy of Spiritual Intercourse, p. 22

...the most wonderful,
beautiful,
and momentous miracle of all miracles,
consists in the development
of those intellectual powers
and spiritual perceptions
in man's immortal soul,
whereby the spirit-land has been discovered
and its vast possessions explored.

Andrew Jackson Davis
The Philosophy of Spiritual Intercourse, p. 33

[of Davis]
The grave-visaged operator ties a handkerchief
about the youth's uneducated head—
closing the world yet more out,
and leaving him to his own psychical changes
and transformations.
Do not turn away your gaze, dear reader,
for the mental crisis has just arrived.
Behold! the inner folds of his intellectual organs
begin to tremble and expand like opening flowers.
They emit a soft atmospheric ether,
which rapidly saturates the air of the room,
and ascends, like the water-spout at sea,
toward the heavens.
What a delicate column of light!
See it arise!—
above the house, above the highest steeple,
above the loftiest mountain, above the pale moon,
above the holy stars, above the reach of telescope,
above—away—higher—beyond all elevation,
save that of the true soul's aspirations!

(continues...)

Yes! can you not see
that radiant shaft of spiral light
reaching all the way from the sleeping youth's uneducated head
to a Focus of Thought beyond the stars?
There! Do you see that?
An answering shaft descends!
His benumbed hands do quiver
with a new sensation,
and the muscles of his face do vibrate and tremble
with the inflowing power....

The scribe set his chirographical hand in order,
and the doctor—who, according to previous direction,
was to pronounce aloud after the low-spoken youth,
to make sure that each word was correctly heard and written—
being also ready,
the clairvoyant slowly
and without excitement
began...

Andrew Jackson Davis explaining his clairvoyance at age 19
The Magic Staff, p. 304-305

[of Quimby]
He seemed to know that I had come to him
feeling that he was a last resort,
and with but little faith in him
or his mode of treatment.
But, instead of telling me that I was not sick,
he sat beside me,
and explained to me
what my sickness was,
how I got into the condition,
and the way I could have been taken out of it
through the right understanding.
He seemed to see through the situation from the beginning,
and explained the cause and effect so clearly
that I could see a little of what he meant.
My case was so serious, however,
that he did not at first tell me I could be made well.
But there was such an effect produced by his explanation
that I felt a new hope within me,
and began to get well from that day.

Annetta G. Dresser describing her first visit with Quimby
The Philosophy of P. P. Quimby, p. 49-50

I remember one day especially
when a panorama of past experiences came before me;
and I saw just how my trouble had been made,
how I had been kept in bondage and enslaved by the doctors
and the false opinions that had been given me.
From that day the connection was broken
with these painful experiences,
and the terrible practices and experiments
which had added so much to my trouble;
and I lived in a larger and freer world of thought....

He seemed to make a complete separation
between the sufferer and the sickness,
and he talked to the sufferer in such a manner
that, gradually, his senses
would become attached to the new life or wisdom
which his words conveyed
instead of the painful sensations;
and, as this continued, the sickness disappeared.

Annetta G. Dresser describing Quimby's healing methods
The Philosophy of P. P. Quimby, p. 49-50

...while in my clairvoyant condition
I seemed to be a sort of connecting link
between the patient's disease
and its exact counterpart (or remedy)
in the constitution of external Nature!
For each visceral or organic deficiency and need in man
(which may be the basis of disease),
I instantly perceived a corresponding agent
of gratification or restitution.
Even so to his every functional, nervous,
or muscular necessity
or demand (which may also become a disease),
I could discover an appropriate and adequate supply.
The existence of this supply, this agent,
this remedy for disease,
I first felt as by an instinctive sympathy;
and then, in nearly every instance,
I would proceed to exercise my power of vision
to see in what field, or book, or drug-store,
the required article was located or described.

Andrew Jackson Davis
The Magic Staff, p. 253

...When a tree is in the twig state
it is not prepared
for the bearing of fruit,
and, therefore,
God procrastinates the bestowment of it
until the tree has acquired sufficient strength
to sustain the weight thereof;
then he prepares,
and attaches to the spreading boughs,
such fruit as in his wisdom
he may ordain the tree to bear....

So, likewise,
it is only proper to say,
that mankind display simply what they
are capable of developing.

Andrew Jackson Davis
The Philosophy of Spiritual Intercourse, p. 27

[Quimby's] difficulties are instructive to us, however,
since they indicate that in thus
gradually learning to keep his own spirit free
by realizing the protective presence of "Wisdom,"
as he briefly called God's power with us,
he passed through a period of analyzing his patient's feelings by
making himself receptive,
allowing those feelings to impress themselves
upon the sensitive-plate of his mind
(his own illustration, drawn
from his experience with photography),
and then comparing them with the Divine ideal.
For this contrast was essential to his Science.
It led the way to his view that
there is a part of us,
namely, the spirit,
that is never sick, never sins;
but is what he called "the scientific man,"
the man of Christ or Science,
in his articles on this subject.

Horatio Willis Dresser, Quimby's biographer
The Quimby Manuscripts, p. 68

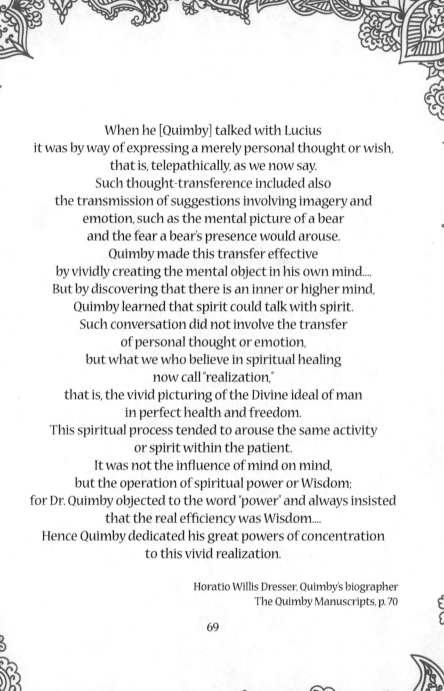

When he [Quimby] talked with Lucius
it was by way of expressing a merely personal thought or wish,
that is, telepathically, as we now say.
Such thought-transference included also
the transmission of suggestions involving imagery and
emotion, such as the mental picture of a bear
and the fear a bear's presence would arouse.
Quimby made this transfer effective
by vividly creating the mental object in his own mind....
But by discovering that there is an inner or higher mind,
Quimby learned that spirit could talk with spirit.
Such conversation did not involve the transfer
of personal thought or emotion,
but what we who believe in spiritual healing
now call "realization,"
that is, the vivid picturing of the Divine ideal of man
in perfect health and freedom.
This spiritual process tended to arouse the same activity
or spirit within the patient.
It was not the influence of mind on mind,
but the operation of spiritual power or Wisdom;
for Dr. Quimby objected to the word "power" and always insisted
that the real efficiency was Wisdom....
Hence Quimby dedicated his great powers of concentration
to this vivid realization.

Horatio Willis Dresser, Quimby's biographer
The Quimby Manuscripts, p. 70

69

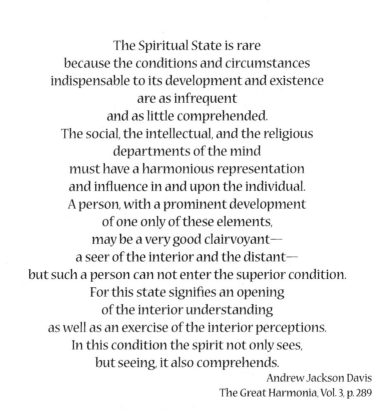

The Spiritual State is rare
because the conditions and circumstances
indispensable to its development and existence
are as infrequent
and as little comprehended.
The social, the intellectual, and the religious
departments of the mind
must have a harmonious representation
and influence in and upon the individual.
A person, with a prominent development
of one only of these elements,
may be a very good clairvoyant—
a seer of the interior and the distant—
but such a person can not enter the superior condition.
For this state signifies an opening
of the interior understanding
as well as an exercise of the interior perceptions.
In this condition the spirit not only sees,
but seeing, it also comprehends.

Andrew Jackson Davis
The Great Harmonia, Vol. 3, p. 289

Wise Counsel

When the mind is substantially in the Spiritual State,
the upper portions of the head are beautifully illuminated!
The superior divisions of the social and the intellectual faculties
are glowing with a bright, mellow light
which centers in the moral faculties,
and this light glows and extends upward about four feet;
the upper portion of which light
is generally about twenty inches in diameter,
and variegated as the rainbow—
indicating the different loves and wisdoms
which are excited by the illuminations....

Into the bosom of this light—the heat of which
a sensitive hand can detect above the subject's head,
when the Spiritual State really exists—
flow the breathings of the love circles or of the wisdom circles,
just as the law of use may at the time prescribe....

Andrew Jackson Davis
The Great Harmonia, Vol. 3, p. 291-292

73

For, should we ascertain
that Man was designed
for some higher and nobler purpose
than that of living, sleeping, eating, toiling, and dying
upon the Earth's surface,
then will we perceive higher uses and more beauties
in the anatomy and physiology of his constitution.
Then will we realize
not only the sublime truth
that the stomach was not made merely to digest food,
the liver to secrete bile,
the heart to circulate the blood,
and the brain to control the body;
but we will discover and contemplate deeper truths—
structure within structure,
function within function—
even a Spiritual anatomy and physiology
of the most magnificent character and momentous import.

Andrew Jackson Davis
The Great Harmonia, Vol. 1, p. 16-17

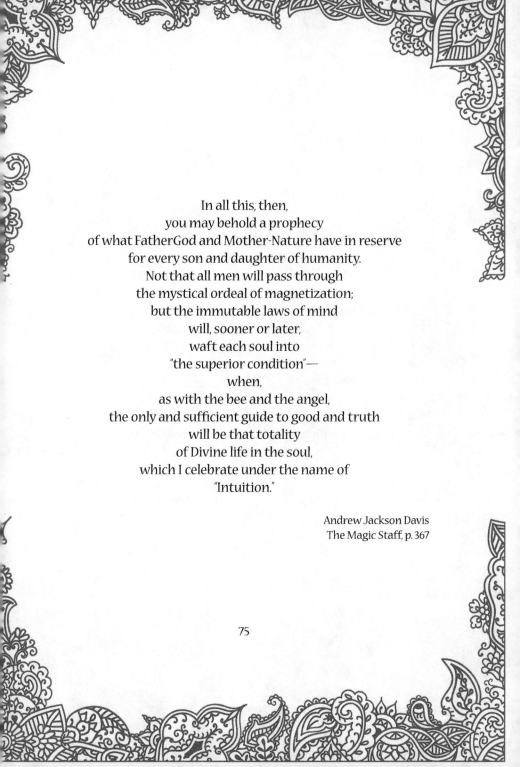

In all this, then,
you may behold a prophecy
of what FatherGod and Mother-Nature have in reserve
for every son and daughter of humanity.
Not that all men will pass through
the mystical ordeal of magnetization;
but the immutable laws of mind
will, sooner or later,
waft each soul into
"the superior condition"—
when,
as with the bee and the angel,
the only and sufficient guide to good and truth
will be that totality
of Divine life in the soul,
which I celebrate under the name of
"Intuition."

Andrew Jackson Davis
The Magic Staff, p. 367

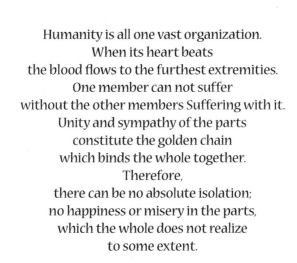

Humanity is all one vast organization.
When its heart beats
the blood flows to the furthest extremities.
One member can not suffer
without the other members Suffering with it.
Unity and sympathy of the parts
constitute the golden chain
which binds the whole together.
Therefore,
there can be no absolute isolation;
no happiness or misery in the parts,
which the whole does not realize
to some extent.

Andrew Jackson Davis
The Great Harmonia, Vol. 3, p. 339

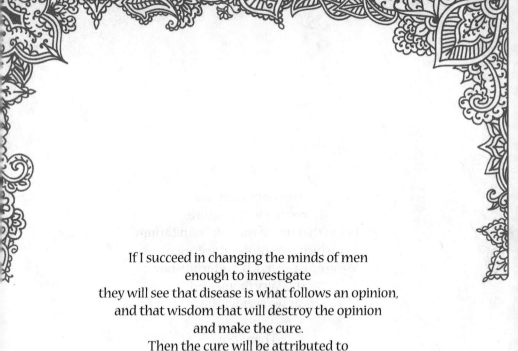

If I succeed in changing the minds of men
enough to investigate
they will see that disease is what follows an opinion,
and that wisdom that will destroy the opinion
and make the cure.
Then the cure will be attributed to
a superior Wisdom,
not a power....

I prophesy that the time will come
when men and women shall heal all manner of diseases
by the words of their mouth.

Phineas Parkhurst Quimby
The Quimby Manuscripts, p. 286 & 277

Live not in the past,
neither in the future;
but in that unmeasurable infinitarium
which constitutes the Present.
We are just as much in eternity now—
this very moment—
as we ever will be....

Therefore,
our "way, truth, and life,"
are distinctly defined.
We must be right in heart and head today
in order to secure a happy tomorrow.
Do what is right under the circumstances.
Do your best!
Be certain that your still small voice—
the angel of your heart—
approves of what you do.

Andrew Jackson Davis
The Great Harmonia, Vol. 3, p. 362

Now, like the latter [the old practitioners],
do not deceive your patients.
Try to instruct them and correct their errors.
Use all the wisdom you have,
and expose the hypocrisy of the profession in any one.
Never deceive your patients behind their backs.
Always remember that,
as you feel about your patients,
just so they feel towards you.
If you deceive them,
they lose confidence in you;
and just as you prove yourself superior to them,
they give you credit mentally.
If you pursue this course,
you cannot help succeeding.
Be charitable to the poor.
Keep the health of your patient in view,
and, if money comes, all well;
but do not let that get the lead.
With all this advice,
I leave you to your fate,
trusting that the true Wisdom will guide you—
not in the path of your predecessors.

Annetta G. Dresser quoting Phineas Parkhurst Quimby
The Philosophy of P. P. Quimby, p. 59

In conclusion
let me urge you to get Wisdom.
This is the great Savior.
Know thyself.
Be the simple-minded devotee of Nature's laws.
Have a good and benevolent Reason for every thing you do.
Never act from a narrow, selfish impulse.
Be loving and tenderhearted.
Always remember that happiness depends upon
physical and mental tranquillity—
upon individual and social harmony.
Never do wrong.
For while I speak,
there are thousands of pure and loving angels looking upon us,
desiring our speedy deliverance
from discord and error.

Andrew Jackson Davis
The Great Harmonia, Vol. 3, p. 230

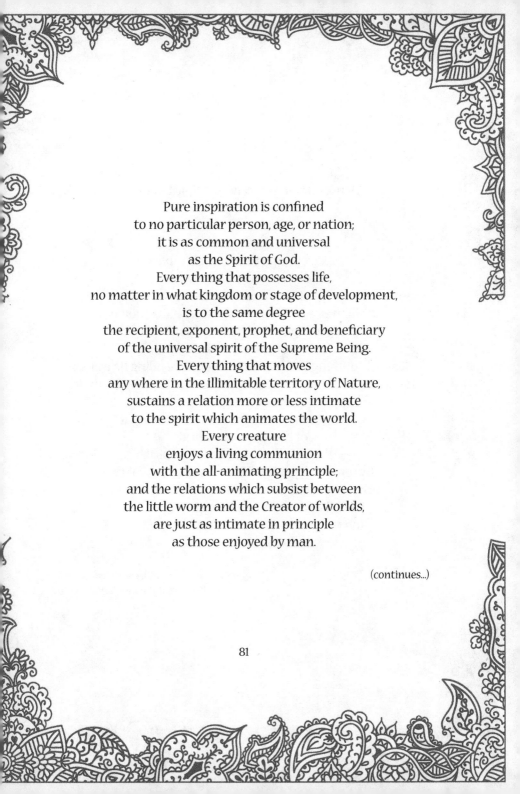

Pure inspiration is confined
to no particular person, age, or nation;
it is as common and universal
as the Spirit of God.
Every thing that possesses life,
no matter in what kingdom or stage of development,
is to the same degree
the recipient, exponent, prophet, and beneficiary
of the universal spirit of the Supreme Being.
Every thing that moves
any where in the illimitable territory of Nature,
sustains a relation more or less intimate
to the spirit which animates the world.
Every creature
enjoys a living communion
with the all-animating principle;
and the relations which subsist between
the little worm and the Creator of worlds,
are just as intimate in principle
as those enjoyed by man.

(continues...)

Hence all things receive the Spirit of God,
and bathe in it,
and express it
in the external,
in exact proportion to their capacity
and absolute requirements....
Man's external organism is closely joined to the material world;
but far more closely is his spiritual nature joined
to that principle which enlivens and energizes
the universal Whole.
There is nothing between man and the bending heavens.
He can bare his head beneath the dome of the living temple,
and there is no obstruction intervening
which can shut him from a contemplation
of the gorgeous fabric.
And so if he will but bare his spirit
by removing pride, selfishness and sensuality,
which circumscribe and entomb its fair proportions,
he will find nothing existing between him
and the enjoyment of that true inspiration
of which I now speak.

Andrew Jackson Davis
The Great Harmonia, Vol. 3, p. 30

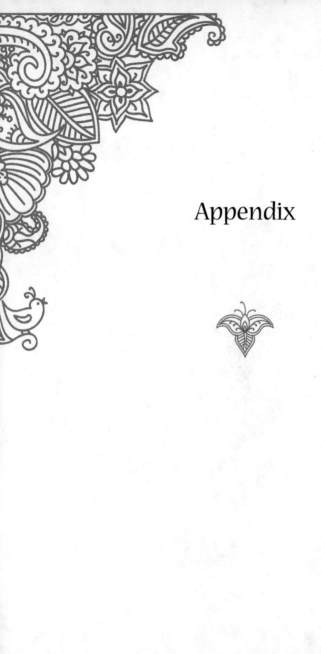

Appendix

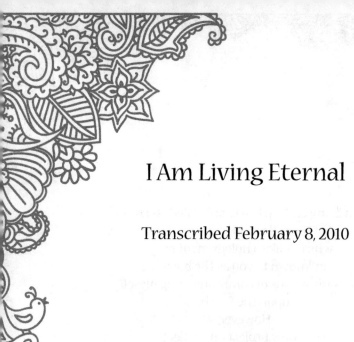

I Am Living Eternal

Transcribed February 8, 2010

I am living eternal in a space called eternity.
The reflection of my life,
which is like a hologram of me,
or known to you as the body,
is my only means of communicating myself
upon the Earth.
However,
I can only project and reflect
upon the physical being (my hologram)
based upon the accepted beliefs of the hologram
and in accordance with the Natural, Moral, and Universal Laws.

Thus the hologram,
my natural, physical being,
has the potential to be anything
in keeping with those laws and beliefs
and merely needs to BELIEVE
in order to affect change upon the natural being
and the perceived surroundings.
The natural being only needs to change a belief
so that I may reflect change accordingly through the being.

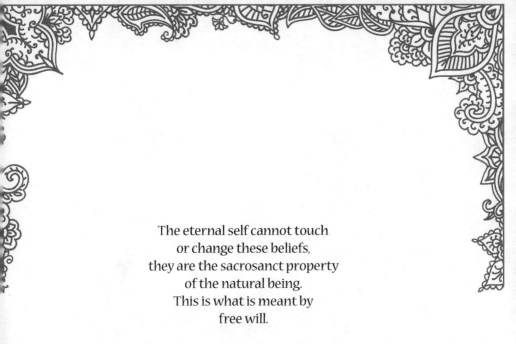

The eternal self cannot touch
or change these beliefs,
they are the sacrosanct property
of the natural being.
This is what is meant by
free will.

The natural being constantly intercommunicates
with the eternal
through beliefs,
which in turn affects the etheric body,
and then the natural body,
in accordance with the beliefs and desires of the natural being.
The unknowingness of the eternal being
is what is meant by
separation.

2/8/2010

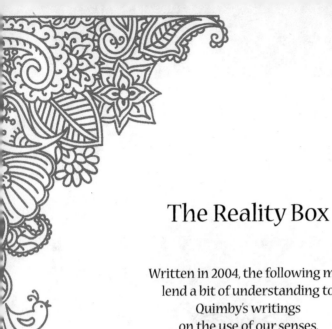

The Reality Box

Written in 2004, the following may
lend a bit of understanding to
Quimby's writings
on the use of our senses.

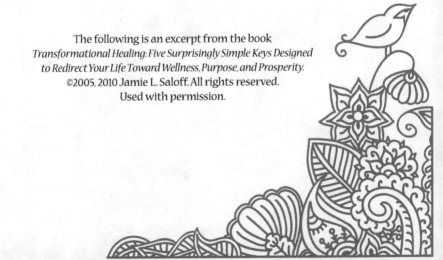

Creative imagination is a kind of bank. Not one that holds money, but one that holds an endless depository of ideas. Tapping into this bank and withdrawing from its holdings is the closest we get to being with God and like God, while living on the earthly plane.

Think of it in this way, no matter what you need, the means to get it are within the imaginative part of your mind. You merely need to reach into the ethereal ooze of thought and pull out a handful.

There are two realms that we accept and understand. One is the realm of reality, the here and now, in this physical world. The other is the realm of our imagination.

For a moment, I want you to think of the here and now, all that's real and in the world, reality as we know it, as fitting into a large, but ordinary, cardboard box. Anything that you know of as real is now in that box. I want you to see the box in your mind as if you are on the outside of it looking at it. You can view it from any angle, turn it in your mind. Just know that all reality, the world, the planets, outer space, everything, fits into that cardboard box.

First, notice that "reality" has boundaries. Nothing "real" can exist outside of that box, so reality can only exist inside the box.

Now, as you look at the box, realize that you are not inside the box (or at least, the thinking part of you). You know that you are not in the box because you are looking at the outside of the box. You can imagine yourself inside the box, but the observer you is not bound by those cardboard box sides. Therefore, you, or the observer you, are existing in a space that is not real (as we define reality).

Secondly, anything you now see existing outside the box is existing in the realm we refer to as our imagination. Whether you imagined your box in a totally blank space, or a white, heaven-like room, or any other countless creative existences, you still know that all reality is in the box and imagination is outside the box.

Play around for a moment with your imaginary realm. Add anything you like to it. You can place your observer self in a room with furniture, you can see yourself standing beside a magnificent mountainscape, or standing in a windblown wheat field. You can add flowers, rain, moonbeams, flying pigs, unicorns, bugs that talk. There are no limits, boundaries, or morally accepted rules because, in this space, it is only imagination.

Continue creating whatever you would like in this space. Even erase it and start again. Feel free to talk to whomever you want, do whatever you please, you are in an imaginary realm. It's kind of like an awake dream. Create art, fly through the air, talk to dead presidents, be wild, be brave, be boundless. Just remember that wherever you are, the box is also there with all of reality tucked inside it. (I prefer to see my reality box as open, with items haphazardly thrown in like a child's toy box and with items coming in and going out of the box, but feel free to simply imagine your box closed if you prefer.)

Now ask yourself one simple question. What if everything were somehow reversed? What if everything in the box, that which we think of as "real," was the dream and everything in the imaginary world was the true reality? By that, I don't just mean the imaginary things you created now, I mean the whole ability to create what you want, the feeling of freedom, of peace, of unbound possibility. Think about that for a moment.

Wouldn't this also mean that whatever was in the box, whatever you put in there as "real," was also a part of your imagination? What if everything you thought of as "real" were part of your imagination? Now,

92

suddenly, "imagination" is not just a child's toy. Suddenly imagination is a kind of nuclear power.

"But wait a minute," you might say, "if we are this being (the observer) who is in charge of our imaginary realm, then how is it we are living in the cardboard box ruled by the limits of its sides and stuck with its physical pain? Why don't we erase all of our hardships and physical limitations?"

Because it is a choice you made, a kind of game you agreed to play when you came here. The only problem about this game is that you are so good at playing it, you have forgotten it is a game. You need a very strong connection and focus to play at this level. In fact, just being here in the "real" world means you are a master at playing the game, what we might call a professional, a person envied by those who are not able to manifest themselves at this level of reality.

However, in keeping your focus on the game and on reality, you've forgotten about all the abilities and powers you have when you're not in the box. You've forgotten that you can be pain free, that you can have whatever it is that you want, that you can be whatever you want.

My purpose in telling you this through a simple, philosophical exercise, is not to stop you from playing the game, because, after all, we have all chosen to play it and enjoy doing so on another, higher level of our being. My purpose is merely to remind you of the power you have available should you choose to use it. A power that allows you to put into your box of reality anything you need to play and "win" your game.

Here is something to get your mind thinking more along these lines and on how to get items from your imagination into your reality box.

What is a rocket ship made of? It is made of imagination. "But how can that be?" you ask. "I see it on the launch pad. I see it in the sky. I know it's made of metal and plastic, tile and wood, painted and molded, bent and smoothed, polished and honed to perfection by countless people over years and years, some who gave their lives so it might be made possible."

But how did it all begin? Someone thought of it in a dream or in a flash of insight. It lived in their imagination. And how did they bring it into reality? They took the idea they saw in their imagination and they wrote it down on paper. They drew pictures of it, first as a whole, then later as pieces and parts that would go into building the rocket. They talked about it to others and shared their vision in such a way that others saw the vision too. Some laughed, but others believed and pitched in to help. There were trials and errors, there were other new inventions brought into being as they were necessary to make the original idea real. And then, there was a rocket ship flying into space as real as anything else in this world.

In this same way, you can make your imaginative ideas real.

1. Write them down or draw a picture of them
2. Share them with others
3. See them in detail with all their parts
4. Act on them to build them or make them happen.

As long as you only dream of your ideas and hopes, and do not carry them any further than that, they will remain in the other, "imaginary" realm. In order to exist inside the reality box, you have to draw them in.

Selected References / Suggested Reading

Andrew Jackson Davis:

The Great Harmonia, Vol. 1, The Physician
The Austin Publishing Co.,
Rochester, NY, 1909, 14th Edition
(First Edition, 1850)

The Great Harmonia, Vol. 3, The Seer
Benjamin B. Mussey, Boston
J. S. Redfield, Fowlers, & Wells, NY, 1852

The Magic Staff
Bela Marsh, Boston, 1867

The Philosophy of Spiritual Intercourse
Colby & Rich,
Banner of Light Publishing House, 1890
(First Edition, 1851)

Views of Our Heavenly Home
A Sequel to: A Stellar Key to the Summer-Land
Colby & Rich,
Banner of Light Publishing House, 1877

Annetta Gertrude Dresser:
The Philosophy of P. P. Quimby
Geo. H. Ellis, Boston, 1895

Horatio Willis Dresser:
Health and the Inner Life
G. P. Putnam's Sons
The Knickerbocker Press, NY, 1906

The Quimby Manuscripts
Thomas Y. Crowell Company, NY
1921, 4th printing
(First Edition, 1859)

Modern Works:

Transformational Healing:
A Self-Healing Journey Toward
Greater Wellness, Personal Growth,
and Purposeful Living
Rev. Jamie L. Saloff
Sent Books, 2005

A Course in Miracles
Dr. Helen Schucman (Scribe)
Foundation for Inner Peace, 1977, 2007

Energy Medicine and
Energy Medicine for Women
Donna Eden, David Feinstein
Jeremy P. Tarcher/Penguin

Phineas Parkhurst Quimby:
The Complete Manuscripts
edited by Dr. Ervin Seale,
DeVorss & Co., 1988

Phineas Parkhurst Quimby:
His Complete Writings and Beyond
edited Ronald A. Hughes,
Phineas Parkhurst Quimby Resource
Center, 2009

Walter Russell:
The Universal One;
The Message of the Divine Iliad Vol. 1 & 2; and
The Secret of Light
University of Science and Philosophy
Waynesboro, Virginia

CPSIA information can be obtained
at www.ICGtesting.com
Printed in the USA
BVHW061053240820
587154BV00011B/902